<u>Foreword</u>

It is my privilege to introduce you to this set of verses.

I have known Andrew for many years and can testify to the honesty shown in these poems.

Andrew is not afraid to admit his fears, self-doubt or loneliness and I am sure all readers will be able to identify with some of these as they are expressed in these verses.

Yet throughout the roller-coaster of emotions the dawn of hope is never far away.

We are left with the surety that; however we are feeling in the moment, darkness will finally give way to light.

N. C. Phillips

Dedication

Deepest gratitude and love to my 2 daughters and my son, without whom I would not be where I am today, and thanks to whom. everything is possible.

My gratitude and deepest thanks go to my editor Norman Phillips, who has been a constant form of inspiration and encouragement to me.

To Gareth L, a friend who is far away but is also very near to me in my thoughts, a friend who has been the voice of reason and hope for me.

My very good friend Will G who has assisted me in preparation of this book, with words of hope and well-being.

There are a number of people that I would like to thank, some from my distant past, some new in my life, but there have been some very close friends that have always been there throughout, to whom I would like to dedicate these poems.

They have lived each of these with me, alongside me. Not always in person, but often in mind and spirit. A few are no longer with us, Phillip H, Paul H and Leon R, I will always have them in my memory, and their legacy is everlasting.

To my very special friend Crawford B, and to a much loved and special person in my life who is not only friend but a brother a son, a mate, Allan S., we've been through a lot together, physically, and mentally. I hope that these poems resonate with you and appreciate you in the journey we have all been through.

Hope

Rises

From

Darkness

A Journey of Emotions Through Verse

Author: A.M. Hall

Editor: N.C. Phillips

To those others I have not mentioned but would dearly like to acknowledge as we have all shared highs and lows throughout our individual and joint journeys.

Life is a rich tapestry, and it's like that never ending rollercoaster. And as the old saying goes, it's not where you start, its where you finish, and how you have made that journey.

Special dedication to the characters and events that I have met and that have helped shape my life and the very personal journey and thoughts that have helped shape me and this book.

To one and all, thank you.

A. M. Hall

CONTENTS

SOMETHING LOW

Is there something I've done wrong
Why do I feel like I have no friends
All I want to do is be nice and kind
Do I do things that are not the trends

I smile at people as they walk past
Everything I do is from good intention
Acknowledge and respect others in life
Why do I feel that I'm in detention

They look at me but look away
I look back to catch their eye
Why did they smile at me earlier
Now they look up towards the sky

Making me feel worthless and unwanted
Are they hiding anything from me
What do they know that I don't
Is there something they won't let me see

Looking at me in a disparaging way
Is there news about me that they know
I feel so down when they look at me
They are making me feel unworthy and low

Mental Demolition

What is it with my Mental Health
Will it be better if I had wealth
The feelings in my head are wrong
No longer do I feel that I am strong

Is there anyone I can talk to about this
Nothing stops me falling into the abyss
Am I too alone too insular to be noticed
At that dark place that is the remotest

I feel as though I'm being attacked
My hopes and dreams have cracked
It's a lonely place that I find myself in
Normal living and life appear in a spin

Darkness descends further on to me
I feel that this is where I'm meant to be
Do I have anyone that I can turn to and talk
I feel afraid to even go outside for a walk

All avenues that I explore appear to be closed
My confidence and happiness have been bulldozed
I cannot understand how to resolve the situation
Feel like I'm in a permanent state of demolition

GROUP BLAME

Surrounded by a group of strangers
I was an outsider and they all knew
Making polite conversation together
How am I supposed to not feel blue

Looking and trying not to stare at anyone
Wanting to join in to be able to just say hi
Wondering if anyone was talking about him
Was it too much to ask before I leave to cry

It's obvious that I'm not in the clique crowd
I don't particularly want to try to be like them
All I want is to be acknowledged for who I am
Maybe this is from where my insecurities stem

I really do not know what I am doing here
Maybe I should just go back to where I came
It looks like another time of sadness for me
But deep down who is it really that is to blame

I Am A Person

I have a voice but I feel scared and frightened to use it
Why do people always want to contradict whatever I say
I'm scared of opening my mouth for fear of being put
down
I curl up into my own world to hide for the rest of the day

I am a person with a heart
I am a person that has feeling
I am a person who feels hurt
I am a person who needs healing

I feel like I'm being walked over like a door mat
I feel that no one listens to me when it does matter
I try my best but I feel like I'm wasting time and effort
My hopes and dreams of helping others seem to scatter

I am a person with a heart
I am a person that has feeling
I am a person who feels hurt
I am a person who needs healing

Do people actually listen to the words that I am saying
Is it me feeling that whatever I do or say is wrong
Do they put me down to make themselves look good
I do not think that will be able to stay in control for long

I am a person with a heart
I am a person that has feeling
I am a person who feels hurt
I am a person who needs healing

Mood Swan

How my mood changes
Like a roller coaster
So happy one moment
Life is not like a poster

What causes these changes
Are these moods just in my head
Am I really changing often
Maybe just spend the day in bed

Psychological problems in me
Solutions are proving to be hard
No support to be had or found
That feeling always being on guard

Investigations are required to help
What is the help that I will receive
Pills and medicine make no difference
Is professional there to help relieve

Physical and mental illnesses arise
Dark depression settles into my soul
I need to find a secluded hideaway
The place is as I dig a big hole

Will I be missed from the vast globe
Does anyone notice that I have gone
Sure no one will search far and wide
Oh to be as free as the graceful swan

LIFE DOUBT

My life felt empty
It now starts to fill
Emptiness fades away
Romance does not kill

At last the mist rises
Albeit in slow motion
Clear skies start to loom
I see the clear blue ocean

It all becomes clear to me
The beauty that is around
The richness that engulfs me
Fulfilment that cannot compound

What can cause this change
Will anything stop me
Things happen we know not why
Happy moments that we do not foresee

Did I dream sweet dreams
Am I imagining good things
Is there an unexplained change
This is what joy and hope brings

Have I discovered I'm worthy
Is this the reality I'm actually in
The change from yesterday
Removing doubt that was built-in

THE INVITING EFFECT

The effect of a bright morning
Weight has lifted from my shoulders
The lack of judgment from others
I feel I no longer carry boulders

People greet me with respect
My demeanour they have viewed
I don't look angry, I look sad
I'm taken aback by their attitude

The spring like day enriches
Many people show joy all around
Most treat you much better
And don't put you in the ground

Give a smile here a smile there
Makes such a difference to us all
Not too much ignoring from now
Let's have more inviting to the ball

AS FAKE

As each day passes
Another day of regret
Another day of hope
Memories need to forget

The new day starts
Hope comes to mind
Friends to be made
New friends we'll find

Looking in the mirror
Hope rises to the top
Life is not that bad
Dreams will never stop

Help is round the corner
At any time of year
Support is there for us
As we face our fear

This is the time
The change to make
Be true to one
No need to fake

EVERYDAY CHOICES

Everyday what do we hear
We hear waste of space
We hear waste of time
But is it really waste

Who says these words
Why do we listen
Our past says what
Our own truth missing

Take a deep breath
Gather a thought
Where you are now
Battles once fought

Inside your own soul
Listen to those voices
What should you decide
Make your own choices

What Rebirth

What do I do now
What do others see
What kind of person am I
What do others think of me

Should I be worried
Should I be concerned
Should I be scared
Should I be perturbed

Is this all there is
Is this what I am
Is this the future
Is this my plan

Do I deserve this pain
Do I deserve this view
Do I deserve this scorn
Do I deserve this hue

How do I get better
How do I get to improve
How do I snap out
How do I get to move

Who am I doing this for
Who am I trying to show
Who am I looking at now
Who am I wanting to know

Don't believe the rumours
Don't believe the demise
Don't believe the looks
Don't believe the despise

Believe in yourself
Believe in your worth
Believe in your friends
Believe in your rebirth

What Time

What is wrong with me
Why do I feel this way
Feeling like I'm a failure
Why do I feel this way

Why can people judge me
Is it just me that feels this way
What have I done for this
Is it just me that feels this way

Have I done something wrong
I wish I knew what it was
I really don't know what's up
I wish I knew what it was

Persecution weighs me down
Should I have these feelings
Is it self-doubt or the truth
Should I have these feelings

Sitting alone in darkness
I feel the tears in my eyes
I do not know if I am good
I feel the tears in my eyes

How do I control myself
Am I alone in this time
I do not know if I can go on
Am I alone in this time

I BEING

I miss the closeness of a hug
I miss the closeness of tenderness
I miss the closeness of a hand
I miss the closeness of togetherness

Being solo can be good
Being solo can be adventurous
Being solo can be exciting
Being solo can be mysterious

I miss the feeling of intimacy
I miss the feeling of loving
I miss the feeling of passion
I miss the feeling of kissing

Being solo is not always good
Being solo is not always glorious
Being solo is not always happy
Being solo is not always joyous

SHINING FEELINGS

The sun is shining brightly
The bright rays glowing on my face
As I lay there thinking of nothing
It dawns on me that I'm in a good place

All the worries are still there
But one by one they start to fade
Not everything is as bad as it seems
The thoughts in my head feel preciously made

Positive thoughts and feelings appear
Edging out the feelings that are bad
Replacing the wrongs with the rights
Replacing the feelings that were sad

One by one the clouds lift above
Not much is left in the way of wrong
There is now a way forward for me
I am there starting to feel so strong

FEELINGS AND BELIEF

Looking around and sitting alone in a pensive mood
Taking stock of his life his decisions as he sipped his drink
Looking around at the wonders of nature and of the world
He stopped to gather his thoughts and let himself think

The beauty and glory that surrounded him
Was a beautiful picture and a blessing to see
It made him forget all his troubles and all his woes
Thoughts about his life and things that were key

Thinking about what deep down was precious
Thinking deeply about his friends and his family
The wrongs done and the mistakes he had made
Coming together to bring him a deep sense of reality

Feelings were coming out, feelings of love
He felt in his heart a strange sense of relief
Bringing him hope, joy, and excitement
For the future, for himself, this was true belief

NEW LOVE

She appeared form nowhere
A fresh breeze is in the air
My life has been enriched
Negative feelings have been ditched

It seems to be a long time
No wedding bells would chime
I've had this same old feeling
That to many I was not appealing

My heart has lifted
New feelings gifted
She is full of grace
Beautiful smile on her face

Didn't think I would feel like this
Not used to feeling this bliss
Thinking of her makes me smile
I now walk with swagger and style

Looking into space and thinking
My heart is no longer sinking
Love that had been removed
Back now my life has improved

SMILE SHELF

I think of her smile
The affection that is shown
The eyes that sparkle
The bond that has grown

I think of her when I go to sleep
And all through the night
When I wake in the morning
My emotions are so bright

My sense of faith has been restored
This lady who has changed my life
Emotionally I am feeling so wanted
Is it too soon for her to be my wife

Now I have a skip back in my step
The best feeling by a country mile
Not needing to be sad and alone
There is a reason for me to smile

My demeanour has changed so much
Daily I chuckle and smile to myself
Now and then I sigh with a deep joy
No way am I going to be left on the shelf

ARE THEY

Are they laughing at me
Are they laughing with me

Are they abusing my good nature
Are they destroying my near future

Are they affecting my physical health
Are they pulling me down by stealth

Are they totally bringing me down
Are they thinking of me as a clown

Are they disrespecting my way of life
Are they cutting me with a knife

Are they making me feel isolated
Are they making my life desolated

Are they trying to control my actions
Are they trying to determine my reactions

Are they deliberately making me sad
Are they deliberately making me mad

Are they trying to make me leave
Are they trying to make me grieve

_Am I_

Am I too nice
Am I easily fooled
Am I too kind
Am I easily ruled

I'm told I should toughen up
I'm told I should be harder
I'm told to treat others bad
I'm told to not show ardour

This is not how I want to live
This is not how I truly feel
This is not how to treat others
This is not the way to deal

What I want to show is love
What I want to show is hope
What I want to do is to respect
What I want to do is to protect

CONSTANTLY FURLED

Constantly I'm feeling alone
I felt my heart was made of stone
But that's not really the case
As you can see by my face

I hear voices in my head
They turn my rage to red
But that is not really me
I'm as calm as the sea

How can I release the pain
Shall I walk down the lane
Clear from my head the bad thoughts
Maybe I should play more sports

What do I really want to do
Is it possible not to feel blue
I need to look hard inside
Help make me show pride

Strange feelings run through me
Buzzing around like the bumble bee
Can I prevent this happening
Is this why my life is baffling

As I try to work it all out
I start to lose the sense of doubt
The wonders of this beautiful world
Negative thoughts are soon furled

LIFE GRIN

She came into my life
From I know not where
A classic vision of beauty
I cannot help but stare

What she sees in me
Is a mystery to unravel
Do I feel worthy of her
Now anywhere I will travel

Like the butterfly that flutters
My heart bounces up and down
She has lifted my spirits so high
I no longer feel like that clown

What a wonderful place to be
It's like I'm floating above the ground
I feel so wanted and loved
This feeling I have has no rebound

I think of her daily
My head in a spin
Her eyes that sparkle
All I do now is grin

New Flow

As the new week begins
I try to cast out all my sins
Feelings for me inside to deploy
That will help to bring me joy

The hope that comes along with it
That will help regain my personal wit
Always looking for that feeling of good
No need for me to hide within my hood

Looking up at the sky that is blue
Feeling that this week will be true
What will this new week to me bring
One hopes that it will make me sing

No weight appears on my shoulders
There is no room for those scolders
Plenty of joyous emotions abound
Infectious feelings flow to those around

RETREATING SOUL

Retreating to my inner sanctum
Is it here that I feel safe and sound
A place of solitude of quietness
I want to be alone and not be found

Am I able to find peace in this place
I feel so alone but here I feel I belong
Blinds pulled as darkness surrounds me
I am away from that busy buzzing throng

No room for others to try to destroy me
Alone with my thoughts and tribulations
Being here trying to figure out my mind
Is it possible to lay new life foundations

Will I be in this seclusion for a long time
When will I know that it is time to leave
How long will I remain in this dark place
Any hope of peace for me to achieve

Thoughts dart in and out of my mind
Many deep dark images fly around
Am I destined to always be like this
What place is my soul now bound

PUSH AWAY

When you find someone special
At first glance you feel that something
How do you show them how you feel
Without doing things ruining everything

How often do you call them
Do you deliver too many messages
What is too many and too few
Where is the light for the dark passages

What is the line for overpowering
Do you stop to think about your actions
What is the message that you are sending
Loss and gain are often dealt by fractions

You continue on your own way
Not realising you are becoming possessive
Sending more and more to them
But are you becoming deeply obsessive

You send more messages without response
Gifts and flowers you continue to send
Do you know what they are thinking about
As you start to drive them round the bend

Words and actions start to lose their value
The other one starts to shift away in defence
Trying harder to get them to respond to
For everything you now do they find offence

How do you learn from this
What to do for the next time
You've pushed this one away
No time for you to shine

COLOURS BRIGHTEN

Different colours that enrich our lives
Shades like yellow green red and blue
And these all help to shape our mood
Create thoughts inside that are new

Shades are here to brighten our day
Mixing our deep and varied emotions
Believing in the goodness that it brings
Taking in serene views of the oceans

As the sun shines on all things in view
Different colours bring an air of grace
Scenery changes as you admire nature
As you feel that cool wind on your face

There is no air of despondency around
As the brighter colours shine through
The darker colours slowly fade away
As the day brightens onto the real you

Spoke Things

They spoke different languages
They came from many places
Meeting together far from home
All with smiles on their faces

Respect for each other was evident
There was no sign of grief or hatred
Greeting each other with a warm grin
Understanding of what to them is sacred

No friction or animosity was caused
Just a general feeling of togetherness
Making new friends and being as one
And what feeling of joy and happiness

How long can they or are they able to stay
What was the reason for them to be here
What if anything will stop this moment
Showing only friendship not showing fear

No one was there to interfere with them
They all got on so well without any fallout
Why can't we all live like this they asked
Are we able to make the bad things dropout

TUNE REQUIRED

Wow that is a great tune
Resonating in my room
It takes me back to a happier time
Where no mountain I had to climb

Living each day in bliss
When is my next kiss
Those days seemed so carefree
Go on a clothes shopping spree

We had music of taste
Food we did not waste
Our fashion at times was dubious
The dance moves were incredulous

Shall we go back there
When we all had hair
With music and films we were alive
We would jump in the car and drive

Oh those good memories
Never needing accessories
The life we had was not complicated
We never needed to be sophisticated

Were we just naive
What did we achieve
Through music we were inspired
No pretence was for us required

PEOPLE PROSE

Why do some people say hello
And talk to you one day
Come the next day they ignore
Walk past without a word to say

Do they think they are better than us
What gives them the right to do that
We feel so low and mistreated
Making us now feel oh so flat

We have good and bad days
Everyone is equal we are told
Equality is for us in all walks of life
But that story never seems to be sold

When they want something they talk
But how do we respond to those
Do we lower ourselves to their level
No, we rise above and answer in prose

TIME BIRTH

Do you have time for thoughts
Do you have time for reflection
Do you have time for peace
Do you have time for affection

Is there time for quiet
Is there time for others
Is there time for rest
Is there time for lovers

Will you have time for yourself
Will you have time for your friends
Wil you have time for your family
Will you have time to make amends

Do you know time is short
Do you know time is unpassable
Do you know time is precious
Do you know time is valuable

How will time affect your life
How will time describe your worth
How will time make you feel
How will time remember your birth

Who Has Been

Who has been there for you when it's dark
Not just who has been there through the light
At the drop of a coin who was there for you
And was there to help you through the night

Remember who it was that listened to you
Who has helped you when times looked bad
When you were feeling lost with no direction
Who was it that helped you when times were sad

Was it someone who is only there when you are rich
Or was it someone who was really there just for you
Who was there to pick you up when you were down
To help you get through the feeling of being blue

Forget those that only come to you when it suits them
It was that person who wanted absolutely no reward
Don't forget who it was that helped you through it all
Who wanted a brighter future for you to go toward

YOU ALONE

You think you find the one
The joy returns to your body
You can't stop thinking about them
You no longer feel shoddy

The spring is back in your step
Your friends notice a change
A purpose has come back now
This new feeling feels strange

You feel happy on the inside
A grin appears on your face
You start to feel complete again
No longer is there empty space

Making plans for the future
Your heart never was stone
The path ahead looks bright
No longer do you feel alone

THE FLYOVER

The head feels misty
Mixed messages that are risky

How can I be relieved
When no one can be believed

Who can I trust
Though that outer crust

I open up my heart
But get used from the start

Names on my phone
But perpetually feel alone

Do I try too hard
I am always on my guard

One day I'll learn
And I will find the right turn

I will be able to smile
If that does not turn into a trial

One day I won't be a pushover
Instead I will be that important flyover

OASIS MEMORIES

Am I sitting in an oasis
I can't believe the beauty
Everything is picturesque
The smells here are fruity

This is how to relax
Wonders that abound
Lazing in this dream
That place I've found

Can anything beat this
The harmony I am in
This cool calm breeze
With no sign of any din

Sun shining on my body
Fortune today is here with me
Places like this are rare
The gentle waves of the sea

Will I come back here
The vision will not leave
I'm not sure if I'll return
Memories I will believe

GOALS IMPROVEMENTS

Setting goals in your mind
Creating opportunities to succeed
Breaking down those barriers
The passion in your heart to feed

What is stopping you to grow
Is there a reason for you to stop
Figures and facts pour into your head
Ease your mind and aim for the top

Looking around for friendly inspiration
Assistance from others is so beneficial
The cycles in your mind create a route
A realistic approach that's not superficial

Feeling the difference before you started
The humour that you now capture each day
Inside your body jumps up and down
Improvements you've made are here to stay

LEAVE FEAR

As those we love to leave our lives
We are always looking who to blame
There are always new people moving in
Even though they are not the same

They are not replacements or substitutes
These are not looking to take their place
Not moving in and removing memories
But to come in and fill the empty space

To provide a new hopeful view on things
Look at life in a different perspective
Bringing hope and friendship and peace
Will they be able to alleviate the negative

Sad as all our feelings may seem to be
We will always remember those not here
Those precious moment that we all shared
Allowing us to face the future without fear

Always See

Always by your side and you by mine
No matter even if anything has happened
We will always be there for each other
Especially in times when we feel saddened

You found me when I was at a low point
My confidence and self-esteem were gone
Picking me up and giving me new strength
There for me with a shoulder to lean on

Not once did you ever ask for anything
Kindness and hope in you were shared
Talking with me in a calming manner
It shows how much that you so cared

I will never forget the very dark times
Without you I could not have survived
A calming influence surrounded my body
Confidence in me was completely revived

You never abandoned at those bad times
What you did for me is difficult to explain
No reward was expected just a smile
Now it's sunny even when it starts to rain

I will never forget those kind deeds and words
All the time you spent looking out for me
And while others left me without any help
You straightened me out for all those to see

BATTLES GIVE

Battles to face on a daily grind
What are the odds of us winning
Support and friends we try to find
Forces together will be twinning

Flying deep in to the unknown
Working out ways and means
Our hands will not be shown
This we inherit from our genes

How do we drive ourselves forward
Can we cope with what will be coming
Or do we take a few steps backward
Trying to avoid pains that are numbing

Are these battles of our own making
Did others create these difficulties
Our souls and health are they breaking
Suffering indignant and vile cruelties

Do we have the tools to deal with this
What armour do we need to fend off
Or will everything turn out to be remiss
Do I just give in and my hat I doff

PEOPLE BLAME

Groups of people standing chatting
Quiet non-eventful Friday night
All around throngs of chats and laughs
Inside himself there is that fear of fright

Wanting to be part of the group
But feeling lonely and out of place
Wishing the night would soon end
Wanting to be in their own place

To see if he could identify anyone
He cast his eye around the room
In a similar state as he was himself
To help lift him up from this gloom

Someone who could help him escape
Get away from this awkward situation
No one wants to make friends with him
Climbing the walls in sheer desperation

Is this a common case for other people
What if there are others who feel the same
Suddenly he starts to gain some composure
Realising that it is not him who is to blame

EYES FIND

That look in her eyes
Persona full of intrigue
Unbelievable vision I see
But way out of my league

Not to everyone's tastes
We all have differing views
Must motivate myself more
How can I reignite my fuse

Inhibitions take over me
My confidence has gone
Unsure about things now
Anything that I can call on

Everything is so difficult
No energy or strength
Feeling out of sorts
Who's on my wavelength

Stuffing knocked out of me
Let down so many times
Unable to show much trust
What do I want to be

Not capable of fun
Lost in the pit of sadness
Trying too hard
Will I find happiness

MIXED SENSE

Is everything all mixed up
Trying to make sense of it all
Confusion seems to reign
I'm definitely not having a ball

Not understanding things
Trying to make sense of it all
Mixed messages I receive
Makes me run down the hall

Can't explain what's what
Trying to make sense of it all
Trying to decipher words
Hope I'm not heading for a fall

What do I not understand
Trying to make sense of it all
Jumbled words in my head
Is making me feel so very small

People treat me wrong
Trying to make sense of it all
My mind is in a spin
Trying to make sense of it all

INSPIRATION HOLES

Inspiration can be found anywhere
Is it impossible or is it improbable
What is it that you want to achieve
Are those visions incomprehensible

Clarity in your mind and wishes
Determine what you want to do
Look for a guiding light to help
Even though it's difficult for you

No need to prove you are better
A self-determined drive is needed
Allow yourself the freedom to grow
All past learnings you have heeded

Like a tree that grows over time
Be patient and set out your goals
There is no rush to succeed in life
Be that person that fills those holes

WORDS PAWN

What do words signify
To you what are they
Make you feel pensive
Or do you want to play

People say words to deflate
And they use them to praise
How do we interpret them
Will your inner spirit raise

Words can be used to be cruel
Deliberately abusing someone
Looking at them sink down
Turning their joy into stone

These abusers are empty inside
They don't care what they say
They act like they are big people
They think they ruined you day

Then you feel the warmth of a smile
A good person says something kind
You feel respected and hopeful again
Positivity drives into your mind

Your day has now improved
Those put you down words gone
Negative thoughts pushed away
No longer are you anyone's pawn

Golden Space

The hair that is golden
The eyes of deep blue
The glow on the skin
The smile that is true

What more could I want
What I want is now here
What can beat this time
What is there to fear

The smile that she brings
The fresh smell of fir
The vision of beauty
The aura that is her

What is it that feels special
What is it that she does see
What can be better than this
What can she not do to me

The sense of being wanted
The smile that is on her face
The love that is in her eyes
The filling of that empty space

BELIEVE HOPING

Losing oneself in a make-believe world
It is one way to face any issues or hurt
But what happen when you return back
Will those painful thoughts simply revert

Always looking around for an answer
Do I bring these problems on myself
Trying to escape the realism of today
Placing them neatly on the highest shelf

All those special days are now spent alone
Losing yourself in some hopeful happy places
Too long have you been there on your own
Remembering the times of joyous happy faces

At times those imaginary places are the best
To lose the painful experiences of every day
Believing that life should be good and hopeful
Hoping to find that place to feel good and stay

DEFINES SOMEONE

What is it that defines who we actually are
Is it how many times that we use the gym
How long we can keep a conversation going
Or what is it we do when we go for a swim

When you look into your soul what do you see
Is it that person who is known for having fun
That always enjoys themselves no matter what
Lazing about and soaking up the rays of the sun

Or are you the one who looks at things in detail
Reviewing everything and never go out on a limb
Take measured steps to look at those problems
The chances of getting things wrong are very slim

Are you the person that is always looking dour
All your contributions seem to amount to none
But deep down do you feel that you are okay
Making sure that all your daily tasks are done

Do solemn vibes emanate from you at times
Is it a feeling you get that there is nothing grim
Mixture of happy and sad thoughts mix around
At any time you feel like you could sing a hymn

When you feel good about what do you do
At times do you say to yourself I'm going for a run
Taking things in your stride by being yourself
And a simple smile when someone calls you hun

With Moderation

Sitting there with another pint in my hand
Who am I trying to convince that I look grand
Is it me thinking that I look like I am the one
Am I simply hiding behind that façade in the sun

Hitting the bottle is not the answer
Just adds fuel to the fire and fervour
What point am I trying to prove
Am I just trying to find my groove

Being popular doesn't mean act like the fools
In my mind I need to find all the right tools
Must try to keep a modicum of self-respect
Positive values are what I should select

Drinking is used by many to black out things
But never making plans for problems it brings
Not saying never again to ever have a drink
But moderation is good so take time to think

THIS MORNING

This morning I wake up with inspiration
This morning a new day begins positively
This morning I am determined to succeed
This morning a new day begins positively

This morning I have a permanent smile
This morning I am in a special place
This morning I know how to react
This morning I am in a special place

This morning I don't need to hide
This morning I can be true to me
This morning I will be good to know
This morning I can be true to me

This morning is a start of a new me
This morning there will be no frown
This morning I will face all my fears
This morning there will be no frown

This morning I cannot be put down
This morning I am happy for all to see
This morning I have that look on my face
This morning I am happy for all to see

DEMONS FLOP

There're demons for me to face
That make me fall from grace
All I do is stare into space
I feel unable to find my place

Is anyone able to win
Either with or without sin
When one can only hear a din
All my dreams go in the bin

Will I find a helping hand
To help me to feel grand
Where is the promised land
On my own feet will I stand

What words do I have to say
Am I able to find a place to lay
Who will let me know the way
Can stillness come into the day

Settle down and harvest a new crop
Gain positives to never stop
Bless the sun and each rain drop
Looks like I may not be that flop

MOOD HEAD

how my mood changes
like a roller coaster
so happy one moment
life is not like a poster

what causes these changes
are these moods just in my head
am I really changing that often
maybe just spend the day in bed

is the drink doing this
but I hardly ever drink
what is affecting me
trying hard to think

sometimes up in the clouds
then I'm down in the drain
why do I feel so mixed up
noises in my head again

POSSIBLE UTOPIA

Is it possible to find things you might get
What is the feeling of Euphoria
Understanding what to do and when
What is the way to reach Utopia

Some things in life you will never get
No matter how hard that you try
Nothing seems to work out for you
Feels that grey is the colour of the sky

Watching other people and seeing them
Look around at people to see what they do
Have they achieved the mindset they want
Knowing that to themselves they are true

To be content in life is a great place to be
Contentment is a form of life I don't know
What is it and where does it come from
Will it help to prevent a state of being low

Achieving what appear to be impossible dreams
Have I now reached that feeling of Euphoria
Sun shining down on me through the clouds
Have I now finally been able to reach Utopia

Scent for All

The scent of flowers that are in bloom
Create an aroma of hope in the room

Where there had once been fear
A path to hope is now clear

Happiness was abundant in the air
No longer was there feeling of despair

The smiles on their faces became infectious
As everyone realised that time was precious

There is no need now to feel down
As it is time to wipe off that frown

Hope is a gift, no matter how small
Peace and happiness are there for all

PRESENT MEMORIES

The past the present the future
Lives with us at all of our time
Where we were are will be
Obstacles in our way to climb

It's not just the sign of our times
How do we shape these things
How do we live these values
In life's rich tapestry of swings

What we thought as precious
Is that still the case these days
And the thoughts we have now
Do they put our minds in a haze

As for tomorrow and the future
What lies in store for you and me
Will we still be friends as we move
Or do we just wait around to see

Yesterday gives us the learning
Today is the chance to create
Tomorrow is the result of now
Put them together we will elate

We have the gift that we know as today
Make the most of the day with no mistake
Yesterday is gone tomorrow is on its way
So let us together special memories make

WONDERFUL SKY

Is everything around me wonderful
Cos my dreams seem so powerful
And they definitely appear inciteful

What is this journey that I have taken
Maybe all others I have not forsaken
It feels like that all good will reawaken

The music is dancing in my head
My feet move to a rhythm instead
The steps of a new beginning I tread

Gone now are those thoughts that saddened
I really do not know what has happened
Where are those feelings that maddened

I do not know where the journey will end
But will I lean to let my feelings extend
Each day a chance to make a new friend

At this moment in time when I do not cry
Look there are no tears in my eye
This makes me feel like I can touch the sky

MEMORANDUM

In fond and loving memory:

Paul

Leon

Phillip

ABOUT THE AUTHOR:

A.M. Hall recently published his first novel; "The Lime Club 16-20",.

A novel based on an historical event in Victorian London that was never solved. Providing an answer to a long-awaited question.

Born in London, into a warm and loving family, the youngest of 5 children. Spending most of his early formative years in between London and Kent.

Very much a family man, father of 3, and holding high family and friendship values.

Music, travel, and sport play a major part in his life. Experiencing many different cultures and ways of life.

Growing up in different places allowing him to discover life's journey and challenges.

Like most people, he has ups and downs in life, which often gives him inspiration to write.

May your hopes and dreams remain intact.

May your hopes and dreams come true.

Never let those fond memories disappear.

Keep looking for good in everything that you do.

Hope

Rises

From

Darkness

A Journey of Emotions Through Verse

Author: A.M. Hall

Editor: N.C. Phillips

Printed in Great Britain
by Amazon

42006632R00046